BY MYSELF

By

D. A. POWELL & DAVID TRINIDAD

Cyself

AN AUTOBIOGRAPHY

TURTLE POINT PRESS NEW YORK 2009

Cyself

To put it in two words: disaster struck. I was born on June 27, 1880, in Tuscumbia, a little town of northern Alabama. I never was coddled, or liked, or understood by my family. My mother's child-bearing had been dangerously botched by a fashionable doctor in New Orleans, and forever after she stood in fear of going through it again, and so I was an only child. It puzzled me a little why Mother had decided to take up butterfly collecting. There was a time when it was thought that she might become a concert pianist. One day, while she was seated at the piano, I ran to her to confess that I had just smashed a cup belonging to her best set of Haviland china. My mother always seemed to me a fairy princess: a radiant being possessed of limitless riches and power. Mother was furious, and I was too—but we had each other, so the hell with it. We knew little about the outside world, having no radio and no TV. That woman never taught anyone anything worthwhile.

2 \ BY MYSELF

12-18 All my early memories, to my mother's intense annoyance, are of the Michigan woods. I made a slingshot to kill rattlesnakes or a bird and I would cook them on a hickory wood fire. It was one of a good many things I learned almost without knowing it; it would be there when I needed it. The Syrians taught me to play knock rummy, in the back of a tiny local restaurant that was closed for regular business but open for pool and card games, so I learned to shoot pool, too. My father was an excellent cardplayer, and his success at the occasional poker game may well have helped to support us. Not having the courage to hold up a bank, or the intelligence to outwit the elite of his own set, he chiseled. And then he was forever going off on his lecture tours, away from us completely for days at a time, because a lecture brought in ten dollars of extra money.

19-27 We lived out of doors most of the time. There were pigs and chickens, as well as Jersey milk cows,

BY MYSELF / 3

from which we got unpasteurized milk, buttermilk, and rich cream. In the summertime, Grandfather wouldn't let us go swimming in Lake Chautauqua without taking along a cake of soap for shampooing our hair and washing all over. Grandfather was a minister in the Episcopal Church. He was a real guru, a gentle giant with big red cheeks and a white beard. Because my father was so rarely around, it was his father whom I called Papa. I don't like to think I was a retarded child, but it is a fact that I was slow. I only know that my thinking went silent, and my sense of self disappeared. After my grandfather's death, my grandmother had come to live with us.

Here is an unflattering story my grandmother told 28-37 me about my early years. I came home from a dancing-school rehearsal distraught because they had taken the role of Cinderella away from me for our Christmas production. Wrapped in my thick bathrobe, I stumbled down the hall. I washed my socks

4 \ BY MYSELF

and ironed my shirt, and put on a pair of sissy short pants Momma brought home from the white folks. I had never seen my grandmother looking so strange. But back then I was worried what this old bitch might tell my mother. They don't make 'em like my grandmother anymore and considering her position on race maybe that's just as well. Grandmother Baxter was a quadroon or an octoroon, or in any case she was nearly white. As a child I used to feel that my grandmother's references to her aristocratic nose were frequently made as an implied comparison with the decidedly snub nose of my mother. She called it the White Ball.

38–45 During childhood I always seemed to be loving boys who didn't love me back. With no sexual experience, I didn't understand erotic obsession or the danger looming over me, yet I sensed that something was wrong and tried to tell my mother. Saying the word *sex* in front of my mother, or even the word *men*, made

BY MYSELF / 5

her shudder with revulsion. Especially during some of the whippings she gave me—and there were quite a few, and they were all different from the whippings I got from my dad. I was so bruised and battered I was afraid to talk. I could see that Mama was trying to act as though she was not worried, but I knew she was. She was visibly upset to my ten-year-old eyes. Probably she realized that opposing me would get her nowhere and would merely exhaust both of us emotionally.

I don't think that I really knew then what sex appeal was—but whatever it was, I seemed to have it. For years I waited in dread for the day my "pee-pee" would turn into this serpent that would snake its way across my room, out the door, and end up God knows where. About my tenth or eleventh year I began to realize that the older boys liked me. Once, walking down the street, I saw a bunch of tough-looking guys dressed in leather chaps and hanging

46–54

6 \ BY MYSELF

all over the parking meters. It is a fact—I zealously guarded my own chastity. This boy flung me down on an upper landing, threw himself on top of me and made me repeat again and again, "No, no, let me go, I don't want it." For me it was like dying and fighting my way back out of the grave. How far is it from that to a bordello in the Casbah? The piercing scream of the mill whistle cut through my reveries.

55–66 In all the seven years I walked to school, no dirty old man ever stopped me for a chat. I was so shy that when walking I'd cross the street if I saw I was going to have to pass someone on the sidewalk. So that I could be closer to home, it was decided that I would change schools the following year. The first day at school was a bit of a disappointment. There were twelve main subjects of study: religion, grammar, composition, literature, history, geography, physics, botany, French, geometry, algebra, and Latin. I was magnificently unprepared. I thought nothing of

BY MYSELF / 7

ducking out a side door and trotting down to the local movie house, on Jefferson Street and Eighteenth Avenue. I could always escape by mooning away about my fabulous future as a movie star. Then I suddenly realized—I don't have any make-up! I was sure that the pounding of my heart could be heard all over the theatre. Someone standing nearby remarked: "God looks after actors. They're his favorite children." A kid doesn't question it when adults tell him that.

My father took me straight over to A. S. Beck's shoe 67-77 store and bought me a pair of black pumps with taps. I felt good when I danced. There was no lack of dancing partners—this town was filled with gay young men. Ian, one of the boys on this circuit, was one of my first boyfriends but, to use today's terminology, it was never a relationship. I was forcing him into a corner, his least favorite real estate, and I could hear the anger in his voice when we went toe to toe.

8 \ BY MYSELF

All I was looking for was a summer romance, which probably would fade in the fall—someone to dance with, to talk to. I looked two days for my man before I could find him, and then I met him coming down the Rio Viejo. The only way I could have had a date with Tex would have been for me to ask him. He complained of having to make any unnecessary move, and when the weather was hot he considered all moves unnecessary. Boy, I was nuts about him. I should add that my affection did not go beyond the costume, and when he took it off I had no time for him at all.

78-89   Back to school. I was approached in the locker room. He was sixteen, gorgeous, a tall, tanned, and handsome farm boy, who looked just like Li'l Abner, only with blond hair. He explained that a prolonged erection without release gets to be painful. He played my young body like a musical instrument, leading me carefully through the act of love until we breathlessly climaxed in a harmony of passion. He began to

BY MYSELF / 9

come by my house on his bicycle every morning before school. The idea was to do it now, do it fast and
get the hell away before the fuzz came. He could
never get enough of that, and I was happy to give it
to him. Mother and Daddy were agreeable as long as
it did not interfere with my schoolwork. My mother
treated him as a member of the family and not only
cooked meals for him but packed chicken dinners,
which he liked for excursions on my father's boat, the
Hully G. I'm convinced that their approach should be
a model for all parents to follow. Duke eventually got
killed when he was hoboing a ride on a train somewhere in Pennsylvania.

The morning after my high school graduation
found me up early job hunting. The only jobs I could
get were the bottom-of-the-barrel scraps that bet-
ter-known men wouldn't touch. I remember I was
very thin that summer, subsisting on shrimp and
vanilla ice cream stolen from the Cockatoo Lounge,
where I worked the breakfast and lunch shifts. These

10 \ BY MYSELF

witty, worldly people were friendly to me. Homo-
sexuals have time for everybody. No doubt that explained the warmth with which I was received: any
diversion was a welcome one. I fit in with them because I knew how to smoke, drink, cuss, and flip off
authority with a disrespectful joke. They spent the
afternoon competing to see who could make the
biggest splash into a murky swimming pool. Twelve
young men, all over six feet, ranging from twenty to
twenty-eight years of age, and not a lemon in the
bunch. Arch and eager, unbelievably affected, I now
spoke with just a trace of transatlantic lisp—in a
voice that had nothing whatever to do with who I
was or where I came from.

100–110 Scouring *Pictureplay* one evening, I was numbed on
reading that the magazine was conducting a beauty
contest for youngsters. I was elated by the idea, but
my first thought was, "What am I going to wear?"
How would the male citizenry react to a man garbed

BY MYSELF / 11

in a flame-colored chiton as I would be that night when I performed my Greek dance? Anyway, here I was, in full cross-dressed regalia, complete with skirt, lipstick, rouge, false eyelashes (how did women ever *wear* those things?), and long flowing brunette wig. I looked like someone on the way to Death Row. The houselights were just dimming down when I saw the auditorium door open in the back and spotted somebody in a familiar old three-quarter-length red coat, standing there, looking around for a place to sit. Fred was a big, handsome man who liked to tell dirty jokes and paw my mother in front of me. "Sparkle," he whispered to me as I went in to the lights and the heat of the cameras. What happened next still makes me laugh. I hit my head very hard and blacked out. Afterward, the audience applauded thunderously.

I was determined to be a movie star. I remember the last thing I did before I left for Hollywood was to stop

12 \ BY MYSELF

at the mirror in the hall and stare at my face. I had white gloves for traveling, and carried my guitar in a plain old cardboard case. It took nearly four days to cross the continent. I had no agent, no manager—I didn't even have a résumé or a headshot. I was skinny and angular and dark, with huge eyes, a funny voice, and a fast, dirty mouth. The only thing I felt good about was my dancing. I turned, I twisted sinuously, I raised my arms languidly over my head, I fell into all the poses of all the sirens I had seen on the screen. Everyone I talked to asked if I was gay or a drug addict or a devil worshipper. I didn't want to say too much, in part because I didn't want to say anything wrong. I didn't talk anyway, and I was pretty good at stunts and pratfalls. I gave myself four months, six at the most, to get an acting job.

123–131   Everyone of consequence in the movie industry had a boat in those days, not only actors and directors but heads of departments, writers and producers. The

BY MYSELF / 13

actors had more fun, they were almost invariably younger, handsomer, and more charming than the bosses. What wondrous nights—youth and beauty dancing to plaintive music on an open-air stage, with the soft sound of waves pounding on the nearby shore. Although we all boozed, none of us ever felt tired or hung over. Finally a call came from Hollywood, but it wasn't from a producer. I sat in my bath with a copy of *Who's Who* on my wet knees. "Would you come to see me?—C.F." was all he said. He was the king! Without quite knowing it, I had set my slingback firmly on the bottom rung of the ladder to Megastardom.

Things suddenly began to happen very fast. I was Big 132–138 Sister, and Nora Drake, and the bad girl on some shows and the good girl on others, and once on *Inner Sanctum* I played a loony elevator man. For a while I danced on *Shindig!*—a rock-and-roll show where the dancers shook their thangs on little podlike stages.

14 \ BY MYSELF

This being radio, we could go to the outer fringes of the imagination at little expense. I just raised my voice above their music and continued to explain about how difficult it was to create an illusion successfully. The idea occurred to me that since we were at the Heigh-Ho Club, and the name was originally an old English greeting, a pleasant radio greeting would be, "Heigh-ho, Everybody!" After all those years of hoping for a big breakthrough, here it was.

139–148 I began to get little parts here and there, and even played a leading role in a segment of a weekly half-hour television drama that appeared every Saturday afternoon called *My True Story*. I was thrilled with the offer because it seems that most adults in the free world watch it every week. The story was basically *Basic Instinct* years before it was made, and is about a hooker who kills all her tricks. All of a sudden I started to be recognised in the street. When I was outed in the tabloids and lost control of my life, I panicked, regressing into the closet. After a while, though, I decided being angry at such stupidity and prejudice was a waste of good time. I also agreed to do a story and be photographed and interviewed for the cover of the December 6 issue of *The Advocate*. There I was, consumed in falls and wiglets, stretched naked across a lynx fur, dripping with Kenneth Lane jewels. A fashionable friend took pity on me and dragged me to Barneys. A few minutes later, I found myself being thrown out into the alley, rubbing my sore shoulder and picking up stray bills that had come loose from my $3000 wad.

It must not be supposed that all my time was consumed in despair and intellectual effort. Let's just say that I didn't let another moment of my prime sexual years slip by unfulfilled. It was open house at Groucho's every Sunday. We all locked arms, and sang Andrews Sisters songs. Improvisational exercises like that can be terrifying but they eventually

149–161

16 \ BY MYSELF

give you a theatrical looseness. One day after I'd sung and gone into a little dance routine I was stunned by complete silence. The silence that surrounded us, as we said and did the funny things that were a part of that script, was eerie. I pretended I hadn't heard; if I hadn't heard, then nobody else had heard. I was a popular companion even when quite young, because of my willingness to climb high into trees. Suddenly I saw two tall poplar trees about ten feet apart immediately in front of us! Reason enough to feel weak in the knees. My knees trembled, but I said with bravado, "Send them up." Sex is an ordeal, or it is a rape, or an athletic endeavor.

162–171   One morning, there was a knock on my door. I was taken into a rather ornate room, when suddenly the Pope came walking toward me. I told him he had better mark the size of it and put his money in his pocket. Something other than the Eternal was present. I believe it was fate. And in spite of my smallness,

BY MYSELF / 17

I decided to accompany him. He kissed me, made the sign of the cross, and turning dramatically as if he were leaving for the Crusades, said, "I'll pick you up at eight." He himself had once been led into temptation and was going home with a woman, but having touched his scapular by chance, saw in a moment an angel waving white wings in air. Her sunglasses attracted a few glances on the street since the weather was so dark and overcast. Certainly she would be in love with him, and now she would look after him and make him happy.

Acting, not prostitution, is the oldest profession in the world. None of us, Marilyn Monroe included, *none* of us could wait to get to work. I made pictures, I made love, and I made martinis. I had no idea of what I was coming across like on the screen—I just knew that what I was doing felt real. Most of those who work in films seem to be sure of what they are doing, though this is only the sureness of medioc- 172–182

18 \ BY MYSELF

rity. In fact, what you have to know how to do is some simple math and, in particular, how to take sights. Back home I sat down with a sheet of paper and made some calculations. I had lost five pounds and already looked a bit better. People judge you by appearances, and since I was all woman underneath, I finally figured I might as well start dressing the part. I lived on welfare, as a young mother out in California, and there was no shame in it for me. For the first time in my life I was beginning to feel I was actually an actress.

183–193 Chameleon tendencies continued in *The Maid's Tragedy*. But makeup couldn't stop this heifer from being clumsy. There one of the greatest surprises of my life awaited me: the bit I was cast for was a colored maid! I was in the picture only a few minutes, but it contained a very emotional scene. We went to our respective dressing rooms and put on our uniforms. I should have quit show business right then

BY MYSELF / 19

and there, but I didn't. I had no intellectual approach, just sheer bloody-mindedness. It was certainly working for the scene, taking my emotional pitch sky-high. Not uncommonly for someone in my situation, I received enough different opinions —about what my role should be, about how I should present myself, about everything that would be or should be expected of me—that I could easily have been ten different people and never satisfied anyone. But to me this was the breaking point. The crew tried their best to comfort me, saying, "It must mean you're going to win the Golden Globe."

I was also nominated for an Academy Award. I was 194–206 happy because it confirmed that I could play complex characters, play against type, and be successful. But be that as it may, everyone wants an Oscar, and the handing out of these coveted trophies takes place at a highly emotional ceremony which makes strong men weak and turns egocentric actresses into

20 \ BY MYSELF

weeping and blushing maidens. I wanted to look elegant. I hung up my big-skirted June Allyson Jewish Princess dresses. The night of the Academy Awards, I dressed in a black lace and gray peau-de-soie gown designed by Irene and was ministered to by Louise, my hairdresser. Every time I see a picture of the dress, I cringe when I remember that I actually paraded around in front of people at that auspicious occasion looking like that. There were thirty-one—count them, thirty-one, stars of the stage and silver screen in the boxes and stalls. Then my name was called. Four and a half hours later, I was *still* onstage. Women's tears always seem to work. We took a break while someone went in search of a dictionary. Well, that kind of loused up that evening.

207–211 My dinner partner was a stunning creature whose name I have forgotten, but who was identified to me as one of Rory Calhoun's ex-wives. She was delighted for me that I had won, and we had a drink to cele-

BY MYSELF / 21

brate, but it was clear that she was tired and wanted to call it a night. But the last time I looked in a mirror, I bore little or no resemblance to Shelley Winters and this is not going to be another "tell-all" autobiography. Through a glass darkly I saw Marlon sitting next to me and said, "Hi," then realized the only place I wanted to go was to the ladies' room. That was probably my greatest moment in pictures—I felt I had really passed the test.

212-222

I was now being paid well for films, and spent far too extravagantly on satin curtains and fitted carpets, not to mention two chandeliers. I was too ashamed to tell anyone. I didn't really need such a large house, nor was it really my style. I didn't want to be by myself in the Hollywood Hills, and because I travel a lot, I wanted someone to watch my animals. Bill dressed with a certain flair; he owned many pairs of Frye boots, which he cared for with loving attention. Then he asked if I'd like to see the gold. Beyond that

22 \ BY MYSELF

little exchange, however, he offered nothing. Then he moved on to Tangier and made, as it were, his name, not to mention literary self, with a good deal of help from Brion Gysin, a brilliant creature, who was to suggest to Bill that what he wrote might be magically enhanced by cutting it up and then piecing together the fragments, presumably at random. I spent the next several days in a kind of trance. I think, time and all its gay amusements and cruel disappointments never appeared so inconsiderable to me before. Stardom, at best, is a tricky status.

223-230 My Hollywood saga wouldn't be complete, however, without mentioning blacklisting. First, I was amused, then angry, and finally frightened at the hatred that poured forth. My arrest and trial were unconstitutional. As both sides anticipated, the real focus of the trial was a battle between psychiatric experts as to whether or not I was insane. It wasn't long before a member of Parliament stood up and demanded that American movie stars stop stealing British children. The motion was denied. The following day the press acknowledged that I had given a creditable performance in what must have been a difficult undertaking. I thought they had no right to judge me or anyone else.

Finally, the opening night of *The End of Sodom* was upon us. The first thing I had to do was check out my equipment. It gave me a feeling of great power to turn on the gas, feel the wind push me backward, lean into it, pull my head down and go like lightning. That's the beauty of live shows. With cat eyes and blond hair and a cup dress pushing up my ass, I'd come out singing "Roll With Me, Henry," "Good Rockin' Daddy," a Ray Charles tune like "Night Time Is the Right Time," and a B.B. blues number like "Sweet Little Angel." The dress showed everything I wanted to hide and hid everything I wanted to show. One man came on foot, with a team of mules, all the

231–239

24 \ BY MYSELF

way from Missouri, wanting me to reveal myself as John the Baptist. I leaped at the offer. And so the incident came to a happy conclusion, effectively giving the lie, I think, to those who insist that Cecil De Mille lacked a sense of humor.

240–255 The journey into addiction has been described so often by so many people in recent years that I don't believe a blow-by-blow account of my particular path would serve any useful purpose. Everybody knows I like buttercream frosting on birthday cake. I was sunk. And then in walks Bea Arthur. I hadn't seen Bea in seven years. She and I performed a very suggestive dance with me blowing away on the saxophone while she climbed all over me. I have always regretted interrupting that experience. Now, like to Eleanor Rigby's grave, nobody comes. I began to get confused and muddled over things. I'd lose weight and gain weight, never enough to make me obese,

BY MYSELF / 25

but I stopped working out. I didn't give a damn what I did, where I went, what happened to me. What the heart held back the anus couldn't: it let out all that was in it. If I had to spend my birthday alone in my room, I was sure as hell going to have a celebration. But after two weeks in there, my stomach went boof! That was my last connection with Earth. I moved the butter.

Many years after this experience, I went to see a psychic in Thailand. This girl there, who later on I found out had several children, all by different fathers, decided to name me as the father of her latest offspring. Having an innate fear of legal documents, I read the affidavit warily. Three days before the hearing, the lawyer called to say he needed more money. I was horrified to learn that each of the ten counts I was charged with was punishable by two to five years in jail and a fine of up to $10,000. Much of it went into

256–263

26 \ BY MYSELF

a trust account guided by a law that required parents to put a certain percentage away for their children. But if you have to work for a living, as I must, what are you to do? Is it any wonder I became known as the "Bag Lady of West End Avenue?"

264-274 I turned down all film offers during this phase, and I filled my time by beginning to write my memoirs. Then I got a call to be guest star on a 1985 series called *Rocky Road*, a call that would lead to a huge turn in my life. I became a hero to a whole generation of children. I knew enough to know that the management and the production would probably be as shoddy and threadbare as it was possible to be, but what did it matter? I threw a make-up towel over the littered shelf and hid a few untidy bits of net and rhinestones. I was then presented with my Arts Caucus Scroll. The Emmy nominations came out—I was nominated for Supporting Actress in a series. But I wasn't a girl any longer. I didn't know, I hadn't any

BY MYSELF / 27

idea. I wasn't a sex maniac, dope user, dog molester, nudist, enemy agent, flag or barn burner, epileptic, leper or vampire. I said I was a witch and indeed I am.

On some very deep level, I had been in denial about 275–286 my health. A hospital seemed cold and impersonal—not to mention the bad lighting. Luckily I still had my underwear on. He was about to lead me through the battery of tests that I knew so well by now that I could have conducted them myself. I didn't question anyone, working as I always used to on the philosophy that "You're the doctor, make me better, tell me how much I owe you and I'll see you around the pool." The doctor wrote a very impressive-looking prescription. He said, "Valium." Wherever I went that fall, I was in a fog. Me, whose most developed muscle is in my jaw. In the middle of an elaborate Italian lunch, I suddenly found tears rolling down my cheeks. When I recovered, I remember thinking it was essential to get myself back into shape; this

28 \ BY MYSELF

was the moment to be fitter than ever before. There is a Chinese proverb that says, "The longest journey must begin with the first step."

287–300 When I was addicted to birthday cakes, I worked out a method for finding out what flavor an uncut cake is on the inside. Unfortunately, that same clarity was missing from my love life. And what I now know is that there are so many questions to which I am never going to know the answer. As far as this book goes, everything is true, even though there are imperfections and certain things that have been left unspoken. After so many years, I've learned to gracefully accept having been so many young men's "first love." When summer has gone and autumn is come I am the flower that welcomes the visitor knowing he never will come. There is, of course, a logic to that. But then there's the bright side of my life, and there's enough good to outweigh the bad. It must have galled the tabloids to see me keep bouncing back, like a child's inflatable clown. I like picnics, babies, sitting on the floor, and playing Santa Claus. I managed to protect my loincloth and my honor almost to the end. And loyalty—I have never found in a human being loyalty that is comparable to a dog's loyalty. The night Byron arrived, Gertrude and I alternately kept him in our laps and when it was time to go to bed Basket could not be found. That is a natural thing, perhaps I am not I even if my little dog knows me but anyway I like what I have and now it is today.

Sources

1 *Memoirs*, Tennessee Williams

2 *The Story of My Life*, Helen Keller

3 *His Eye Is on the Sparrow*, Ethel Waters (with Charles Samuels)

4 *An Unfinished Woman*, Lillian Hellman

5 *My Life So Far*, Jane Fonda

6 *Colleen Dewhurst: Her Autobiography* (written with and completed by Tom Viola)

7 *Lulu in Hollywood*, Louise Brooks

8 *My Early Life: 1874–1904*, Winston Churchill

9 *By Myself*, Lauren Bacall

10 *Lakota Woman*, Mary Crow Dog (with Richard Erdoes)

11 *When Do I Start?*, Karl Malden (with Carla Malden)

12 *In the Arena: An Autobiography*, Charlton Heston

13 *I'm Still Here—Confessions of a Sex Kitten*, Eartha Kitt

14 *One Writer's Beginnings*, Eudora Welty

15 *The Raw Pearl*, Pearl Bailey

16 *Lana: The Lady, the Legend, the Truth*, Lana Turner

17 *Early Havoc*, June Havoc

18 *Laura Z: A Life*, Laura Z. Hobson

19 *Memories*, Ethel Barrymore

20 *Personal History*, Katharine Graham

21 *Love, Lucy*, Lucille Ball (with Betty Hannah Hoffman)

22 *Me: Stories of My Life*, Katharine Hepburn

23 *The Good Life*, Tony Bennett (with Will Friedwald)

24 *Girl Singer: An Autobiography*, Rosemary Clooney (with Joan Barthel)

32 \ SOURCES

25 *Something Like an Autobiography*, Akira Kurosawa

26 *Shattered Love: A Memoir*, Richard Chamberlain

27 *Nostalgia Isn't What It Used To Be*, Simone Signoret

28 *Memoirs*, Andrei Sakharov

29 *"Don't Fall Off the Mountain,"* Shirley MacLaine

30 *My Side: The Autobiography of Ruth Gordon*

31 *nigger*, Dick Gregory

32 *Growing Up*, Russell Baker

33 *Lady Sings the Blues*, Billie Holiday

34 *Early Plastic*, Bill Reed

35 *I Know Why the Caged Bird Sings*, Maya Angelou

36 *Along This Way: The Autobiography of James Weldon Johnson*

37 *Ghost of a Chance*, Peter Duchin

38 *Bog-Trotter: An Autobiography with Lyrics*, Dory Previn

39 *The Million Dollar Mermaid*, Esther Williams

40 *Tab Hunter Confidential: The Making of a Movie Star* (with Eddie Muller)

41 *The Measure of a Man: A Spiritual Autobiography*, Sidney Poitier

42 *Memoirs of a Bastard Angel*, Harold Norse

43 *Only the Strong Survive*, Jerry Butler (with Earl Smith)

44 *Life Lines*, Jill Ireland

45 *Goodness Had Nothing to Do with It*, Mae West

46 *My Life in High Heels*, Loni Anderson (with Larkin Warren)

47 *I'm a Believer: My Life of Monkees, Music and Madness*, Mickey Dolenz (with Mark Bego)

SOURCES / 33

34 \ SOURCES

70 *Jean Shrimpton: An Autobiography* (with Unity Hall)

71 *My Father's Daughter*, Tina Sinatra (with Jeff Coplon)

72 *Where Have I Been?*, Sid Caesar (with Bill Davidson)

73 *Life of Tom Horn, Government Scout and Interpreter*, Tom Horn

74 *Debbie: My Life*, Debbie Reynolds (and David Patrick Columbia)

75 *My Wonderful World of Slapstick*, Buster Keaton (with Charles Samuels)

76 *Veronica*, Veronica Lake (with Donald Bain)

77 *Rex*, Rex Harrison

78 *Jerry Lewis: In Person* (with Herb Gluck)

79 *Will*, G. Gordon Liddy

80 *Sing a Pretty Song …*, Edie Adams (and Robert Windeler)

81 *Somebody to Love?*, Grace Slick (with Andrea Cagan)

82 *Playing the Field: My Story*, Mamie Van Doren (with Art Aveilhe)

83 *Daybreak*, Joan Baez

84 *Going My Own Way*, Gary Crosby (and Ross Firestone)

85 *I Feel Good: A Memoir of a Life of Soul*, James Brown

86 *As I Am: An Autobiography*, Patricia Neal (with Richard DeNeut)

87 *Castles in the Air*, Irene Castle (as told to Bob and Wanda Duncan)

88 *Sally: Unconventional Success*, Sally Jessy Raphaël (with Pam Proctor)

89 *Miles*, Miles Davis (with Quincy Troupe)

SOURCES / 35

90 *Dancing in the Street: Confessions of a Motown Diva*, Martha Reeves (and Mark Bego)

91 *Ed Wynn's Son*, Keenan Wynn (as told to James Brough)

92 *Moving Pictures*, Ali MacGraw

93 *I Remember It Well*, Maurice Chevalier

94 *The Naked Civil Servant*, Quentin Crisp

95 *Force of Circumstance: Vol. 1, After the War*, Simone de Beauvoir

96 *Little Girl Lost*, Drew Barrymore (with Todd Gold)

97 *Cybill Disobedience*, Cybill Shepherd (with Aimee Lee Ball)

98 *Wide-Eyed in Babylon*, Ray Milland

99 *Knock Wood*, Candice Bergen

100 *Tallulah: My Autobiography*, Tallulah Bankhead

101 *The Times We Had*, Marion Davies

102 *One Thousand and One Night Stands*, Ted Shawn (with Gray Poole)

103 *Growing Up Brady: I Was a Teenage Greg*, Barry Williams (with Chris Kreski)

104 *Ava: My Story*, Ava Gardner

105 *One More Time*, Carol Burnett

106 *Life Is Too Short*, Mickey Rooney

107 *Changing*, Liv Ullmann

108 *'Tis Herself: A Memoir*, Maureen O'Hara (with John Nicoletti)

109 *On and Off the Ice*, Dorothy Hammill (with Elva Clairmont)

36 \ SOURCES

SOURCES / 37

38 \ SOURCES

SOURCES / 39

1 6 6 *Aretha: From These Roots*, Aretha Franklin (and David Ritz)

1 6 7 *Evita: In My Own Words*, Eva Peron

1 6 8 *Swanson on Swanson*, Gloria Swanson

1 6 9 *The Autobiography of William Butler Yeats*

1 7 0 *Timebends: A Life*, Arthur Miller

1 7 1 *Ingrid Bergman: My Story*, Ingrid Bergman (and Alan Burgess)

1 7 2 *Brando: Songs My Mother Taught Me*, Marlon Brando (with Robert Lindsey)

1 7 3 *Intermission*, Anne Baxter

1 7 4 *Vanity Will Get You Somewhere*, Joseph Cotten

1 7 5 *Limelight and After*, Claire Bloom

1 7 6 *Fun in a Chinese Laundry*, Josef Von Sternberg

1 7 7 *Long Time Gone*, David Crosby (and Carl Gottlieb)

1 7 8 *Vanessa Redgrave: An Autobiography*

1 7 9 *Change Lobsters and Dance*, Lilli Palmer

1 8 0 *Martina*, Martina Navratilova (with George Vecsey)

1 8 1 *Book*, Whoopi Goldberg

1 8 2 *Natalie: A Memoir by Her Sister*, Lana Wood

1 8 3 *Beginning*, Kenneth Branagh

1 8 4 *Coal Miner's Daughter*, Loretta Lynn (with George Vecsey)

1 8 5 *At 33*, Eva Le Gallienne

1 8 6 *An American Life*, Ronald Reagan

1 8 7 *The Rock Says ...*, The Rock (with Joe Layden)

1 8 8 *I'm with the Band: Confessions of a Groupie*, Pamela Des Barres

40 \ SOURCES

1 8 9 *Broken Music*, Sting

1 9 0 *Send Yourself Roses: Thoughts on My Life, Love, and Leading Roles*, Kathleen Turner (in collaboration with Gloria Feldt)

1 9 1 *Leap of Faith: Memoirs of an Unexpected Life*, Queen Noor

1 9 2 *The Happy Hooker: My Own Story*, Xaviera Hollander (with Robin Moore and Yvonne Dunleavy)

1 9 3 *Burnt Toast*, Teri Hatcher

1 9 4 *No Bed of Roses: An Autobiography*, Joan Fontaine

1 9 5 *Still Me*, Christopher Reeve

1 9 6 *Memoirs of a Professional Cad*, George Sanders

1 9 7 *Married to Laughter—A Love Story Featuring Anne Meara*, Jerry Stiller

1 9 8 *Enter Talking*, Joan Rivers (with Richard Meryman)

1 9 9 *Ginger: My Story*, Ginger Rogers

2 0 0 *Call Me Anna: The Autobiography of Patty Duke* (with Kenneth Turan)

2 0 1 *Every Other Inch a Lady*, Beatrice Lillie (with John Philip and James Brough)

2 0 2 *A Paper Life*, Tatum O'Neal

2 0 3 *A View From a Broad*, Bette Midler

2 0 4 *The Kid Stays in the Picture*, Robert Evans

2 0 5 *My Life in Three Acts*, Helen Hayes (with Katherine Hatch)

2 0 6 *A Book*, Desi Arnaz

2 0 7 *An American Life*, Jeb Stuart Magruder

2 0 8 *One Man Tango*, Anthony Quinn (with Daniel Paisner)

2 0 9 *It Wasn't All Velvet*, Mel Tormé

SOURCES / 41

42 \ SOURCES

2 3 0 *Child of Satan, Child of God*, Susan Atkins (with Bob Slosser)

2 3 1 *Memoirs of a Star*, Pola Negri

2 3 2 *The David Kopay Story: An Extraordinary Self-Revelation*, David Kopay (and Perry Deane Young)

2 3 3 *Wayfaring Stranger*, Burl Ives

2 3 4 *Secrets of a Sparrow: Memoirs*, Diana Ross

2 3 5 *Rage to Survive*, Etta James (and David Ritz)

2 3 6 *Who's Sorry Now?*, Connie Francis

2 3 7 *Take Me Home*, John Denver (with Arthur Tobier)

2 3 8 *Too Much, Too Soon*, Diana Barrymore (and Gerold Frank)

2 3 9 *Bulls Balls Bicycles & Actors*, Charles Bickford

2 4 0 *Cash: The Autobiography*, Johnny Cash (with Patrick Carr)

2 4 1 *Things I've Said, but Probably Shouldn't Have*, Bruce Dern (with Christopher Fryer and Robert Crane)

2 4 2 *The Moon's a Balloon*, David Niven

2 4 3 *If I Knew Then What I Know Now ... So What?*, Estelle Getty (with Steve Delsohn)

2 4 4 *My First Five Husbands ... And the Ones Who Got Away*, Rue McClanahan

2 4 5 *The Good, the Bad, and Me*, Eli Wallach

2 4 6 *Dolly: My Life and Other Unfinished Business*, Dolly Parton

2 4 7 *Counting My Chickens ... And Other Home Thoughts*, The Duchess of Devonshire

2 4 8 *Agatha Christie: An Autobiography*

SOURCES / 43

249 *Tony Curtis: The Autobiography*, Tony Curtis (and Barry Paris)

250 *My Wicked, Wicked Ways*, Errol Flynn

251 *The War: A Memoir*, Marguerite Duras

252 *Be My Baby: How I Survived Mascara, Miniskirts, and Madness or My Life as a Fabulous Ronette*, Ronnie Spector (with Vince Waldron)

253 *I, Tina*, Tina Turner (with Kurt Loder)

254 *John Glenn: A Memoir* (with Nick Taylor)

255 *Hollywood*, Garson Kanin

256 *A Lotus Grows in the Mud*, Goldie Hawn (with Wendy Holden)

257 *to BE, or not … to BOP*, Dizzy Gillespie (with Al Fraser)

258 *Patty Hearst: Her Own Story*, Patricia Campbell Hearst (with Alvin Moscow)

259 *There Are Worse Things I Could Do*, Adrienne Barbeau

260 *Dream Doll: The Ruth Handler Story* (with Jacqueline Shannon)

261 *Still Growing*, Kirk Cameron (with Lissa Halls Johnson)

262 *Myrna Loy: Being and Becoming*, by James Kotsilibas-Davis and Myrna Loy

263 *I Could Have Sung All Night*, Marni Nixon (with Stephen Cole)

264 *Will There Really Be a Morning?*, Frances Farmer

265 *Grace is Enough*, Willie Aames and Maylo Upton-Aames (with Carolyn Stanford Goss)

44 \ SOURCES

266 *Rickles' Book*, Don Rickles (with David Ritz)

267 *Act One*, Moss Hart

268 *Gypsy: A Memoir*, Gypsy Rose Lee

269 *Is That It?*, Bob Geldof (with Paul Vallely)

270 *Hold the Roses*, Rose Marie

271 *Silent Star*, Colleen Moore

272 *Life Is a Banquet*, Rosalind Russell (and Chris Chase)

273 *The Wind At My Back: The Life and Times of Pat O'Brien*, by himself

274 *Sophia Living and Loving: Her Own Story*, Sophia Loren (by A. E. Hotchner)

275 *Breathing Out*, Peggy Lipton (with David and Coco Dalton)

276 *By All Means Keep on Moving*, Marilu Henner (with Jim Jerome)

277 *My Name is Love: The Darlene Love Story*, Darlene Love (with Rob Hoerburger)

278 *Lucky Man: A Memoir*, Michael J. Fox

279 *Am I Blue?*, Elaine Stritch

280 *Life with Jackie: The Personal Story of Jacqueline Susann*, Irving Mansfield (with Jean Libman Block)

281 *Just One More Thing*, Peter Falk

282 *Betty: A Glad Awakening*, Betty Ford (with Chris Chase)

283 *Trying to Get to Heaven*, Dixie Carter

284 *Mayflower Madam: The Secret Life of Sydney Biddle Barrows* (with William Novak)

SOURCES / 45